AVAILABILITY OF TRANS S0-ACB-940

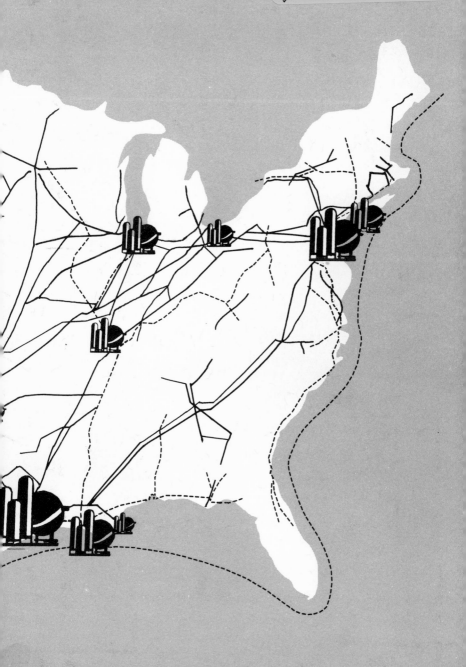

GASOLINE PRICES
AND COMPETITION

GASOLINE PRICES
AND COMPETITION

HAROLD M. FLEMING

APPLETON-CENTURY-CROFTS

Division of Meredith Publishing Company
New York

Copyright © 1966 by Meredith Publishing Company

Library of Congress Catalog Card Number: 65-26736

6125-1

CONTENTS

PREFACE

Gasoline prices, like the prices of many other commodities, are not easy to understand. Sometimes gasoline price wars seem to spell intense competition. At other times motorists, seeing the same prices to the decimal at nearby stations, may think they are up against conspiracy. Or again they may see across the street a price difference between a familiar and an unfamiliar brand and wonder what it means.

This is understandable. The whys and wherefores of gasoline pricing are of almost infinite variety. And they keep changing. They involve behavior patterns beyond the powers of the most fertile imagination. Despite this difficulty of comprehension, it is beyond doubt that the intense competition in the business has brought about a record of reasonable prices. In 1964 the average price of gasoline, not including taxes, was 7 per cent less than it was ten years before. And the 1964 variety was much improved.

Anyone can have such facts—by digging. They have been spelled out in lengthy books and thousands of pages of legislative hearings. Perhaps no business has had its pricing habits so much investigated.

But few motorists have time to read these books, and few people with an interest in the subject of gasoline pricing have time to attend the hearings.

Anyone should be able to get the story briefly. That is what this book is for.

The book may also be of interest to students of economics because the gasoline market is a classic study of the joint influence of large capital investment, "reach for volume," and relatively inelastic demand. The gasoline market has changed a great deal in the last ten years. In many ways it has paralleled the change in American retailing generally. There is a slogan:

Gasoline's a buy—
only the tax is high.

While this does not scan very well as poetry, the sentiment is understandable. With the federal tax at 4 cents and state taxes averaging 6 cents, Washington and the state governments get half as much from the motorist as the whole oil industry, including crude-oil producers. The tax is almost equal to the combined shares of the refiner, the transporter, the wholesaler, and the retailer.

However, taxes are not the province of this book. So all costs and prices discussed here are *before* taxes, except where noted.

This book could not have been written without the financial support of the American Petroleum Institute. But the views, train of thought, and occasional strong statements are solely the author's.

HAROLD M. FLEMING

Antrim, New Hampshire
December, 1965

GASOLINE PRICES
AND COMPETITION

CHAPTER I

THE GEOGRAPHY
OF GASOLINE

Gasoline—A Long-Distance Traveler

The motorist who has just driven a thousand miles might be interested to know that the gasoline he next buys has probably traveled as far as he has, and perhaps farther.

The first important fact about gasoline is geography. Gasoline is one of the travelingest of all basic commodities. Two thousand miles from oil field to refinery to service station is nothing unusual.

The Country's Four Biggest Refining Centers

More than half the country's gasoline comes from four big refining areas.

The biggest—in fact the biggest in the world—is the

refining area along the Texas and Louisiana coast. Here more than 30 refineries gulp over 3,000,000 barrels* of crude oil a day from oil fields near and far.

Ten of these Gulf Coast refineries have individual capacities of at least 100,000 barrels per day. Any one of them could supply the gasoline requirements of more than 2,200 average-sized service stations. Of the ten, five have individual capacities of over 200,000 barrels daily. Of these five, three handle over 300,000 b/d (barrels daily).

The country's three *next* largest refining areas do not hold a candle to the Gulf Coast area. But they are large.

(a) The Philadelphia area—nearly 900,000 b/d;

(b) The Los Angeles-Bakersfield area—over 850,000 b/d;

(c) The Chicago area—about 600,000 b/d.

Nearness to Crude Oil vs. Nearness to Customers

The huge and long-established refinery cluster on the Gulf Coast developed because it is near large, reliable, long-term sources of crude oil and half a dozen giant crude-oil pipelines converge on it from the Mid-Continent and West Texas oil fields.

The newer Philadelphia refining area also developed, partly, because of crude-oil sources. It has deep-water facilities for receiving crude oil brought by low-cost, leviathan tankers.

But the Philadelphia-area refineries along the Dela-

---

* A "barrel," in the oil business, is 42 gallons.

ware River have another major asset: a densely populated market nearby. Fifty million people live within 300
miles of these seven refineries.

Mother Nature inconsiderately put most of the nation's crude-oil resources far from its population centers.
There never has been enough crude-oil production near
Chicago to meet that area's needs; for 50 years it has
been drawing crude by pipeline from the Mid-Continent
area.

But Chicago, like the Delaware River, is in the middle
of a populous area, a big market not only for gasoline
but also for the other products that are made along with
gasoline—home-heating oils, diesel oils, and the heavier
fuels that go into the boilers of factories, mills, and power
plants.

In Los Angeles, Mother Nature was somewhat con-
siderate. Here some refineries sit not only right over oil
fields but near populous, fast-growing markets.

The Rest of the Country's Refining Capacity

There are four other important refining areas in the
country, located near population, not near sources of
crude oil. They are around New York, St. Louis, San
Francisco, and Seattle.

Add these to the Big-Four areas and you have ac-
counted for two-thirds of the country's gasoline supply.
The remaining refineries are widely scattered—partly
(particularly in the Rocky Mountain area) for reasons
involving distance and freight costs.

States without either plentiful crude oil or populous

3

markets are notably short of refineries. Of the six New England states, only one, Rhode Island, has a petroleum refinery. In the Rocky Mountain area neither Idaho nor Arizona has one.

Tankers, Pipelines, Barges

From the country's major refining centers, gasoline moves in millions of barrels per day to nearby and distant terminals.

It goes mostly by three forms of transport, as different as the whale, the elephant, and the salmon that swims upstream.

The oldest of these is the ocean tanker—the whale. From the Gulf of Mexico, tankships carrying an average of 152,000 barrels of refined products move around Florida and up the Atlantic seaboard, discharging cargo all the way up the coast. On the Pacific Coast, tankers move in a steady flow from the Los Angeles refining area north to San Francisco, Portland, Oregon, and Seattle.

"Product" pipelines—the elephant—were first built in the 1930's, though crude-oil lines had been then running for over 50 years. Today, more than 55,000 miles of product lines, in diameters up to 36 inches, move about 3,500,000 b/d of petroleum products, including gasoline, from refinery centers to product-line terminals as far as a thousand miles away.

Latest to become important among the heavy-duty carriers of gasoline to market have been the inland-waterway barges—the "salmon that swim upstream." A single tug can push at one time as many as a dozen of these barges (usually called "tows"). They move along the Mississippi and Ohio Rivers, the Columbia River from Portland, Oregon, the Tombigbee and Warrior Rivers from Mobile, Alabama, and the Hudson River and Erie Canal in New York State. They also move through the Intracoastal Canal from Texas to Florida, from the Georgia Coast to Chesapeake Bay, and up the Sacramento River from San Francisco Bay. This movement increased greatly between the 1930's and the late 1950's.

Competition at the Terminal

These three kinds of massive transport—ocean tankers, product pipelines, and inland-waterway barges—often compete. On the West Coast, for instance, gasoline barged up the Columbia River from Portland to Pasco meets gasoline by pipeline from Rawlings, Wyoming; from Billings, Montana; and from Salt Lake City, Utah.

And in the East, upstate New York can get its gasoline either by product pipeline from the Philadelphia area (connected also with the New York City area), or by river barge up the Hudson and through the Erie Canal, or by lake tanker from Michigan and Ohio refineries. The gasoline marketer has similar alternatives in many other areas.

Freight Cost vs. Refining Cost

There is considerable competition between big refineries and little ones. Geography often plays a role. It is no accident, for instance, that the immense Rocky Mountain

5

area is supplied with gasoline mostly by small refineries, running 30,000 b/d and under. The larger refineries, with the economies of large-volume runs, can afford to ship gasoline a long way by tanker, barge, or pipeline. But, as with other industries, there comes a point where freight costs eat up the economies of big production. It is this that gives the little refinery its place in the system. The freight cost problem shows up particularly just east of the Continental Divide. If it were not for this area's "magnificent distances"—or if freight were free—a single 300,000 b/d refinery could supply every motorist in six Rocky Mountain states—Montana, Wyoming, Idaho, Utah, Colorado, and Nevada.

The "Fan-out"

When gasoline finishes its large-volume trip by tanker, pipeline, or barge, it is discharged into a "terminal"— marine, river, or pipeline. It is most of its distance to market. But it still has its most expensive trip to take— from terminal to service station.

The movement of gasoline from the nation's 273 operating refineries to over 211,000 service stations resembles the upward movement of sap in a tree. It moves up the trunk, out through the branches, and finally into the twigs. And as the gasoline is dispersed, its flow is no longer measured in *barrels* but in *gallons*.

Through the 1920's most gasoline moved from the terminal by railroad tank car out to local "bulk plants." And from these it was hauled by trucks and wagons to its final destination.

6

In the 1930's and 1940's, however, rail movements of gasoline were largely replaced by highway (trailer truck) movements. Big trucks now often take the product to the bulk plants; smaller trucks to the service stations.

In the 1950's and early 1960's improved roads and equipment innovations made possible "Clipper" trucks, named after the fast transatlantic "Clipper" ships of the early 1800's. These now operate hundreds of miles a day on regular schedules. Sometimes they are able to by-pass completely the intermediate bulk plant and take their loads directly from the terminal to the service station.

End of the Trip: The Service Station

The fan-out ends at the service station. Refineries produce gasoline, and tankers, pipelines, and barges move it in *millions* of gallons. Highway trucks and railroad tank cars move it in *thousands* of gallons. Service stations sell it *gallon by gallon.*

Service stations vary in every conceivable way. In some parts of the country there are portable stations, called "skids," that merely sell gasoline without providing water, air, or any service but maybe a kind word. One of these will usually have an "office" no bigger than a phone booth. But at other stations, located in shopping centers, a motorist can park his children in a nursery and possibly take a swim.

The number of service stations in the country has not changed much in ten years. But their locations have changed considerably. And since total annual gasoline sales across the nation were 64 per cent greater in 1964 than ten years earlier, average service-station volume has increased quite a bit.

Station size is often rated by monthly gallonage. The smallest sell less than 10,000 gallons a month; and some of the biggest up to 500,000 gallons.

Flow and Timing

It is a happy peculiarity of petroleum products, among basic commodities, that they *flow*. This makes the oil industry the envy of many others. Coal men experiment with long-distance conveyors. Steel mills can keep their product liquid only from blast furnace to open hearth. Automobile plants move their cars along assembly lines. But none of these industries can make their products flow, physically, all the way into the customer's possession.

One result is that most gasoline is never seen by a human eye from the time it leaves the ground as crude oil through the time it is burned in the motorist's engine.

Another result is that a modern refinery, in contrast to most mills and factories, appears motionless.

Oil companies, to make the most of the peculiar attribute of flow, have had to invest heavily in their *own*, specialized, one-purpose transport equipment. They have spent half as much on this in recent years as on refineries.

Few other manufacturing industries have this burden— or opportunity.

But the fluidity of gasoline and the costly transport system impose a unique requirement on gasoline marketers.

Not only must the product be kept *moving*, but its

8

movement must also be *timed* as precisely as possible to the *right outlets, in the right volume.* If this isn't done, the line backs up, figuratively, to the refinery (or even to the oil field), and the extraordinary economies of continuous flow, obtained at such large capital cost, may be lost.

CHAPTER II

WHO'S WHO
IN GASOLINE MARKETING

MULTIPLICITY AND DIVERSITY

Now that we have seen how gasoline gets to market, let us take a look at who gets it there.

A motorist might assume, by reading service-station signs, that there are perhaps a hundred companies in the business.

And a Russian official or central planner might assume, since gasoline has to be kept on the move, that the signs must actually be disguises for a single monopoly, such as the Soviet's *Soyuzglavneft,* which handles all of Russia's oil and gasoline business.

In this country, however, there are about 12,000 firms primarily engaged in the storage and wholesale distribution of gasoline, oil, and other products.

But this is only in what might be called the middle of

the business. In addition there are more than 10,000 producers of crude oil; some 140 different refining companies; numerous companies specializing in the transport of petroleum products, including gasoline; and at the final distribution end, about 211,000 retail gasoline dealers.

Participants in the business fulfill every conceivable function or combination of functions. Some gasoline moves to market in the hands of a single firm which finds and produces the crude oil, refines it, transports it, and sells it at wholesale. But other gasoline goes through many hands. It may be manufactured by an independent refiner from crude oil supplied by an independent producer; then it may be sold through a broker to an independent wholesaler. Some firms perform only one function; some combine two, three, or four.

And like the voyagers in Noah's Ark, the firms handling gasoline vary not only in make-up but also in size. There is room in the business for firms that represent both very small and very large investments. In fact, measured by money put into the business, the biggest firms are about a million times as large as the smallest.

Thus the following are the size of the chips it takes to obtain entrance:

Small Service-Station Dealer	$ 3,000
Small Jobber	60,000
Large Jobber	300,000
Small Refiner	3,000,000
Small Integrated Company	30,000,000
Small "Major"	300,000,000
Big "Major"	3,000,000,000

THE SUPPLIERS OF WIDELY KNOWN BRANDS OF GASOLINE

The largest factors in the gasoline business are the firms whose brand names are most familiar to the interstate motorist.

Integration

Most of these companies are at least partially "integrated." A few are fully "integrated." "Integration" refers to operating at several levels; for example, owning crude-oil production, refineries, and distribution. In short, a fully integrated company handles the product "from drilling site to service station driveway." Many of the oil firms familiar to the motorist own shares or partnership interests in crude-oil and product pipelines. Some own or contract for the use of tankers and river barges. Most own terminals. Many have or rent railroad tank cars and highway trucks.

This kind of integration is unusually developed in the gasoline business, because the product has to be kept on the go through a long series of operations. Nevertheless there are in practice no companies so fully integrated that they do all their own producing, refining, transporting, and marketing. There are about 50 companies called, by courtesy, "fully integrated." But none are so balanced as to refine only their own crude, and then move and market only their own products. At times all have to sell here and buy there, in the open market.

12

Competition among the Majors

Competition among gasoline suppliers continued to intensify during the 1950's and early 1960's as suppliers expanded their operations and made inroads into each other's marketing territories.

Such expansion was nothing new in the business; but it was on a large scale in the 1950's and 1960's. All elements in the business were anxious to take advantage of the growth in the demand for petroleum products in all sections of the country. Thus a big Pacific Coast supplier moved into the Atlantic seaboard market; while several Eastern, Southern, and Midwestern suppliers joined the competition in the fast-growing West Coast markets.

In this intensified struggle for the motorist's dollar, a dozen among the biggest companies "restructured" their marketing channels. There was a widespread redesigning of brand *signs*. Some companies found that their station signs, though perhaps easily identified by the motorist at 30 miles per hour, were not so obvious at 50 or 60 m.p.h. So color, shape, and symbol were changed.

Also some large suppliers, owning well-known brands in different areas, started gradually to substitute a single brand for them all, so that coast-to-coast and border-to-border motorists would recognize the familiar brand.

As a result, by 1964 five of the largest suppliers were spread so wide they were each selling in 45 states or more; while twelve others were each selling in at least 20 states.

But, for the motorist, the important result was that by 1964 there was an average of 29 gasoline brands being offered in competition in every state of the continental United States. The least offered in any state was 14. The most was 47.

Each gasoline brand usually has its own particular make-up in matters of manufacture, proportions of different hydrocarbon cuts, additives, and so forth. All together, the specifications may fill pages.

A driver, though, almost never sees the product he is buying, and anyway he couldn't judge its qualities simply by seeing it. He has to take someone else's word about a brand—at least until he has had some experience driving with it. He can't evaluate gasoline at all while buying, as he can an automobile in a showroom, so he often buys by brand.

Though only a score or so of suppliers are called "majors," there are additionally over threescore other integrated or partially integrated "independents" selling their brands here and there in the United States—each known only in the South, or in the East, or in the Middle West, etc. Some of these are "big frogs in little ponds" —doing more business, and better known, in their own marketing areas than are the nationally known majors.

Many of these firms are comparatively new. They are usually the achievement of a successful jobber who has "integrated backward" (bought or built a refinery), or of a successful refiner who has "integrated forward" (bought or built a marketing organization), or even of a crude-oil producer who has gone forward into refining and then marketing.

14

THE BRANDED GASOLINE JOBBER

Suppliers' Varied Outlets

A driver seldom buys a familiar brand of gasoline directly from the company that made it. Even the service-station dealer may not have bought it directly from the company.

Refiner-suppliers have several ways of getting their branded products to motorists. It is only in very rare cases that they deliver them to the service station and themselves run the station. Much more often they deliver and sell them to the dealer who runs the station. But there is a third and very important route by which refiners often get branded products to a station. They may sell it to an independent wholesaler, commonly called a jobber in the oil trade, who then handles the last stages of the fan-out from terminal or bulk plant to service station.

In such case the brand name is generally unchanged. The jobber's name or that of his firm may be totally unknown to the buying motorist.

Often the jobber may himself operate some stations, in addition to selling to others. Still he keeps the supplier's brand name.

The Jobber's Marketing Skills

In deciding whether to sell direct or to go through a jobber, the refiner-supplier has an important economic decision to make. Can the jobber, who is an independent local businessman, do a better job of distributing the brand and keeping it up front in the competition? Or can the refiner-supplier itself do a better job through salaried employees?

This final stage of distribution often involves many special local conditions, chances, dangers, and opportunities—as we shall see in a later chapter.

The problems are to store the gasoline as briefly as possible, to move it as economically as possible, and to distribute it as widely as possible.

The successful jobber has a day-to-day knowledge of local prices, markets, road conditions, and delivery methods that may be hard for the supplier company, from a distance, to match. Being a small businessman, he is also likely to perform more tasks himself rather than to hire others to do them; thus he reduces his costs.

He has a further advantage over the salaried company marketer—in small cities and in rural areas. He has lived there a long time. He knows almost everybody. He is usually active in the Chamber of Commerce and other community organizations. He "belongs."

What Is a "Typical" Jobber?

Jobbers usually are not firms but individuals. And they come in an infinite variety. Some jobbers distribute over a few square miles and some over an area as large as New England. Their net assets may range from $50,000 to over $5,000,000.

Most jobbers have bulk plants. But some don't. Some own and operate service stations; some only sell to them. But some do both.

Most jobbers handle not only gasoline but also heating oils, diesel oils, lubricants, and other petroleum products. A few stick to gasoline only.

In 1961 the *National Petroleum News* tried to sketch a composite jobber. He had been in business 20 years; owned four service stations and supplied 15 others; had 134 farm accounts, 936 heating-oil accounts, and 20 commercial accounts.

A typical jobber's chief assets, regardless of what his books say, are his personal contacts and his know-how.

Commission Agents

Refiner-suppliers also occasionally distribute their branded products in other ways. These are varied. One is through a "commission agent." Unlike the jobber, who buys the supplier's branded gasoline outright and resells it, footing all the local distribution costs, the commission agent only handles it as the supplier's agent. He is generally paid a commission of so much a gallon.

THE RETAIL GASOLINE DEALER
"John Smith, Proprietor"

When a motorist pulls into a service station bearing a familiar brand name, the chances are slight that it is either supplier- or jobber-operated. Small or large, it is most likely run by an independent businessman, or proprietor. He almost certainly has his name on the door, or above it.

This man is not an employee. He is self-employed. He

17

buys his gasoline from the supplier (or jobber) and sells it on his own account, to his own profit or loss.

It has not always been so. In the 1920's most companies ran their stations on a salaried basis. It was in the middle 1930's that most large suppliers decided they could do better by selling to local dealers for resale. (The initial spur to the change to dealers was the threat of a state chain-store tax in Iowa. It would have meant higher costs to suppliers with chains of salaried outlets, so dealer operation was tried. The plan proved to have such overall advantages that it spread far beyond its place of origin.) Today, most major suppliers operate only a handful of stations with salaried employees, mostly to provide places where they can experiment with marketing techniques and train dealers. Some suppliers have service stations run on a commission basis. But the total number of such stations is small compared with the number of stations run by dealers who are independent businessmen.

Who Owns the Station?

The independent dealer arrangement, however, involves one big problem. Even a modest-sized station today may cost $50,000; a well-located station in many a suburban or urban area will often represent an investment of three to four times this amount. It is hard to find men with not only the ability to *run* such stations but also the ability to *raise such capital*.

So the means of building such stations and turning them over to dealers are varied and ingenious. Often a local investor puts up the money to build a station on the strength of a lease from an oil company of perhaps 20 years. The company, after leasing the station on long term from the investor, turns around and leases it for one to three years to the dealer.

There are dealers, though, who raise their own money and build their own stations.

The Dealer's Total Business

Inextricably woven in with the dealer's gasoline business are his other lines of trade. Probably most important of these is "TBA"—the trade term for tires, batteries, and accessories. The dealer may also offer repair services; he may even run a parking garage on the side. Sometimes these things will outweigh gasoline sales in revenue importance.

The Supplier and the Dealer

Dealer-supplier relations are necessarily close. The dealer wants to do business with a company that will treat him fairly, keep him supplied with a good brand of gasoline at competitive wholesale prices, and back him up with advertising and promotion. On the other hand, the company wants to do business with a dealer who is capable, solvent, and ambitious to sell a large volume of products.

No supplier is so big or has such a powerful brand name that it can be arbitrary with dealers. As in any retail business, good dealers are hard to come by—and they are constantly sought after by other suppliers. No dealer, though, no matter how strong his community standing, can remain successful if he leans back in his easy chair, relaxes, and lets the quality of his service run down.

Most major-brand suppliers try to help their dealers through financial assistance; advice on bookkeeping and management; absorption of the cost of, and taking the risk on, gasoline credit cards; advertising; sales promotion; dealer magazines; and advice on current marketing techniques.

What It Takes to Be a Dealer

To succeed as a dealer, a man must have the qualities of any successful independent businessman.

He must be willing to work hours that are sometimes very long.

He must have an understanding of successful merchandising techniques and be able to get along well in his personal relationships.

He must be orderly. Few things can go to pieces faster than the housekeeping of a service station.

He must understand the importance of bookkeeping and record keeping. There isn't any other way for him to know how well—or poorly—he's doing.

Supplier companies are constantly looking for such men. If they think a man "has the makings," some companies will start him on a salary in a *company-owned and operated service station,* then help him finance a station of his own. Some suppliers figure to spend as much as $1,500 to develop a good prospect into a good dealer.

NEW COMPETITION

Rise of the "Independent Marketer"

The first part of this chapter described in rough outline what, by the end of the 1940's, had become the conventional, traditional structure of the gasoline business —built largely around suppliers, jobbers, and retailers.

But mass marketing of gasoline has been constantly subject to change—and notably to the entry of new participants.

In the 1950's a new episode was added to the story. It was the rise of the "independent marketer."

In the 1950's and early 1960's there came into existence literally scores of *marketing companies*—some of them operating hundreds of service stations. Generally, they did not have their own refineries, though a few were integrated refiner-marketers.

Twenty years ago "independent marketers" such as these did less than 5 per cent of the country's gasoline business. By 1963 they had carved out 25 per cent of the total market—and it was a market 286 per cent larger.

There is often a Horatio Alger quality to the growth of the new gasoline-marketing chains. Many of them are the lengthened shadow of a man—in some cases of brothers. Some started with a "hole-in-the-wall" station or two, then acquired a third station, a fifth, a tenth, and so on. By 1964 there were 15 of these "independent" marketing chains large enough so that each operated in ten states or more.

Some Nomenclature in the Trade

In the language of the trade the well-known brand-name gasolines of the major companies are said to be "branded gasolines." All others were once called "unbranded," but with the growth of the "independent marketers" new terms have come in, such as "independent brand," "private brand," or "local brand."

"Major" vs. "Independent"

In the early days of the business there were no "majors." But any firm not a part of the old Standard Oil trust was an "independent." (Some of these "independents" have grown considerably bigger in 50 years than several of the now-unrelated companies—some still using the Standard name—that were created from the pieces of the trust broken up under a 1911 Supreme Court decision.)

The term "major" came into being in the 1920's. It meant a big, integrated company. (One of the Standard trust's toughest pre-1911 competitors still calls itself a "major independent.")

A "major," generally, means a company that is both *big* and *integrated*. It must be both. Thus there are integrated companies in the business with assets of only $50,000,000 or $100,000,000. They are not big by oil-industry standards, so no one calls them "majors." On the other hand, there are companies in the oil business, particularly in crude-oil production, with assets in the hundreds of millions of dollars, but stubbornly *un*integrated. So they, too, are not "majors."

As for the term "independent," it is generally applied to any firm that is small, or new, or unintegrated. Each generation of oil men has applied it to newcomers in the business; and so it applies particularly to the marketers who are neither among the many descendants of the broken-up Standard Oil trust, nor big in assets, nor integrated.

Where Do Independents Get Their Gasoline?

"Independent marketers" buy their gasoline from a variety of sources. They have proved as adept in their buying as in their selling.

In a very few cases they have "integrated backward" and bought their own refineries. But rarely have they found it necessary.

Understandably, they buy in considerable volume from independent refiners, many of whom do not have their own marketing outlets.

But they also buy some of their gasoline on the "open market." Such markets exist in all the country's principal refining and consuming areas—the most important of which is the "Gulf Coast market." The gasoline for sale is not necessarily standing still in a tank farm. It may be aboard a tanker in the Gulf moving toward a port somewhere on the Atlantic seaboard, but still for sale.

Into such open markets are offered lots and cargoes from both independent refiners and, occasionally, from the refineries of major refiner-suppliers.

It is no secret that the "independent marketers" buy substantial quantities of gasoline from some major refiners—either directly or in the open market.

Majors in Disguise

Just as manufacturers have in other lines, a few major gasoline suppliers have themselves gone into the private-brand business. One method is to set up a wholly owned subsidiary, which gets its gasoline mostly from the parent company, but sells under a new and different brand. Another method is to buy a private-brand marketing firm.

Outsiders Enter the Fray

In the late 1950's fresh competition from ranks entirely outside the petroleum industry began entering the retail gasoline market. Retailers from entirely different fields formed this new competition. Some felt they could beat the gasoline marketers at their own game. Some began selling gasoline as simply another item in a widely diversified line of goods. These competitors included food chains, discount houses, and mail order houses. Most of them figured to capitalize on the trend toward "one-stop shopping."

CHAPTER III

ESTIMATING THE COSTS OF GASOLINE

A LOOK AT THE PUMP

How Much, and for What?

The gasoline pump face usually shows three things: (1) the price per gallon (to tenths of a cent), (2) the number of gallons rung up (to tenths of a gallon), and (3) the total bill.

Some motorists make a note of how much they paid in total; possibly how many gallons they bought; and perhaps the mileage on the speedometer when they stopped for gasoline. (This can tell them later how many miles they are getting to the gallon.)

But there are drivers who cannot even recall, a half-hour later, the price paid per gallon.

Probably, depending on time, place, and quality, it was somewhere between 25 cents and 35 cents for regular grade, including about 10 cents in taxes. It might sometimes be higher because of unusual circumstances such as short-term seasonal volume of business, remoteness from source, or sparseness of traffic.

Throughout the United States, federal and state taxes make up a big part of what the driver pays. On the average these taxes add about 50 per cent to the price of gasoline.

To illustrate, let us say that the price without tax is a rounded 20 cents. To this is added the federal tax of 4 cents and an average state tax of 6 cents—making the total tax 10 cents.

This means that of the 30-cent price paid by the motorist, only 20 cents is left to go to the dealer, wholesale distributor, the transporter, the refiner, and the crude-oil producer, in short, the whole industry.

At 20 cents a gallon (not including tax) the motorist is getting a basic commodity at a pretty reasonable price. A gallon is four quarts, and weighs about six pounds. At a nickel a quart, it is cheaper than distilled water. At 3¼ cents a pound, it is cheaper than the lowest-cost of all metals—steel. And something that will push a ton-and-a-half vehicle a mile (besides powering its brakes, its steering wheel, and even its windows) for a little more than a penny is reasonably inexpensive energy.

WHO GETS WHAT?

It is difficult to estimate how the price the motorist pays for gasoline divides up between crude-oil producer, refiner, transporter, wholesaler, and retailer. This is so because cost and price factors vary widely in different situations all along the line.

Differences in Costs

Most of the differences in the effort and expenses required to deliver a gallon of gasoline are due to a combination of several factors—local economics, population density, and geography. For instance:

1. The biggest refineries can be built only where there is either a big market to supply or access to low-cost transportation. Such refineries can be both built and operated at an outlay of about two-thirds as much (per barrel-day of output) as small refineries. This means that refined products are likely to be more expensive to produce in the sparsely populated mountain and plains areas not having access to cheap transportation.

2. Where refineries are located in the midst of large population, bulk transport costs by water or pipeline to terminals may be relatively small per gallon.

3. Where terminals are close to dense populations, the fan-out costs from terminals to service stations may be small per gallon. But where population is thin,

hauls have to be long, and so transport costs per gallon are large.

4. Where stations are small and remote and traffic is light, handling costs per gallon sold at the station are much higher than at stations doing a consistently heavy volume of business on busy highways.

Crowded Cities vs. "Magnificent Distances"

For these reasons, gasoline generally costs less per gallon to produce and move in densely populated areas than in the nation's great open spaces. The Rocky Mountain areas are particularly affected. Even where such areas have their own refineries, their sparse markets mean that the refineries can have only a fraction of the capacity of the "large, economy-sized" refineries in the Gulf Coast, Philadelphia, Chicago, and Los Angeles areas.

Also, the mountain areas do not have water transport, one of the most economical methods of moving oil and oil products. And in some cases their markets are too scattered and thinly populated to justify product pipelines, another inexpensive way to move gasoline. The product, therefore, may have to go by rail or highway —the most expensive forms of long-distance gasoline movement.

Lastly, in mountain areas people generally live in small, widely separated towns, where service stations, in turn, have to be small. A notable exception is the densely populated and highly competitive Denver area, where gasoline distribution costs are consequently much lower.

But while geography has a strong influence on gasoline prices, its effect is not always measurable "as the crow flies." For instance Maine, without refineries of its own and the farthest continental state away from the oil country, nevertheless gets its gasoline delivered to terminals cheaper than many inland states, because it is directly supplied by low-cost ocean tanker. In the fan-out from the terminals in Maine, though, sharp differences show up. Such coastal cities as Portland are of sufficient size to permit volume economies in handling from terminals to service stations. But the fan-out to the sparsely populated areas upstate presents a different story.

All such considerations as distance from terminals and population density can sometimes go out the window in trying to figure why gasoline prices are less in one place than in another.

The cause may simply be a marketer, little or big, who has chosen to cut his price in an effort to win new customers—and thus kicked off a widespread price war. But a full discussion of this factor is left to Chapter V.

JOINT COSTS
The Deceptive Simplicity of Gasoline Cost Figures

Many people think that the cost of refining a gallon of gasoline should be fairly easy to estimate. Actually, the problem is complex.

To begin with, gasoline is a "joint product." It is made along with other petroleum products, such as kerosine, home-heating oils, diesel fuel, and even "residuals" such as Bunker C oil, coke, and asphalt.

In this sense refiners are like sheepmen, part of whose product goes for wool and part for mutton. Or they are like meat packers who convert a steer into everything from sirloin steak to glue.

The essential problem of costing joint products is to allocate among them costs of raw material, equipment, salaries, and so forth—and it defies precise solution.

It may astonish the layman that refiners cannot give any exact figure on the per-gallon cost of producing any refinery product, such as gasoline, but only a hypothetical one. The oil stream, on its way through the refinery, goes through much the same equipment, and yet what comes out are many totally different products. So if the refiner asks his accountant how much his gasoline costs, the accountant has a problem to give an answer.

One way is to figure your total refining costs; then subtract the part of those costs you recovered by selling the products *other* than gasoline (allowing yourself a little profit). Then what is left is the cost of the gasoline you sold.

Another way is to figure what you got for selling everything, from which you figure the percentage of that total which you got from gasoline. Then apply that percentage to your total *costs*. That gives you your cost *for gasoline*.

These and other methods are, in a sense, circular reasoning and the answers are bound to be "iffy."

GASOLINE LOGISTICS AND PER-GALLON EXPENSES

The costs of handling gasoline from the refinery gate to the customer's tank are a little easier to figure. It is a clear fact, for instance, that gasoline handling expenses normally get bigger and bigger as the product gets farther from the refinery and nearer the customer—that is, "as the sap runs up the trunk, out through the branches, and into the twigs." Per-gallon costs are low at the beginning of the trip to the customer and increase toward the end.

Below is the way one company has looked at it.

REALISTIC RANGE OF PER-GALLON EXPENSES
REFINERY TO MOTORIST

Bulk Transport	"Fan-out"	Service Station
1¢	1¢–4¢	3¢–7¢

At the Beginning—Mass Movement

The low per-gallon expenses at the beginning of the journey are achieved by mass transport.

They are the result of capital investments in huge ocean tankers, river tows, and product pipelines.

Bulk transport can move the product perhaps a thousand miles to the terminal for a cent a gallon.

An ocean tanker, perhaps 750 feet long and displacing

31

50,000 deadweight tons, costing between $6,000,000 and $12,000,000, may move the gasoline to market.

Or a tug will push a river "tow" of from two to eight barges, each containing perhaps 840,000 gallons of gasoline, hundreds of miles up one of America's rivers to markets far inland.

Or a product pipeline, two or three feet in diameter, costing millions of dollars, may push the gasoline across valleys, hills, and mountains.

Though overall costs of these various means of transportation are high, quantities handled are so enormous that per-gallon costs are very low.

At the End—Time Is Money

But near the end of its trip the gasoline must go by some combination of highway truck, railroad tank car, small-diameter product line, and local truck. The scale of equipment and size of investment necessarily drop, but the per-gallon costs necessarily rise because of the much smaller quantities and much greater handling involved.

Finally, after a brief sleep in the tanks of the service station, the gasoline is dispensed to customers, gallon by gallon. And costs now increase very sharply. From the station's underground tanks, the gasoline's movement of a few yards into the motorist's tank costs on the average about a nickel a gallon. This is five times the entire expense of moving a gallon of gasoline 1,000 miles to a terminal by bulk transport.

Perhaps a single factor will help to explain. Every

minute of a station attendant's time costs money. And every minute is not occupied by serving customers. So some of the time between customers has to be included when figuring the labor cost of filling a gasoline tank. The dealer has other costs too: rent, equipment, light, power, etc.

Savings in Mills, or Tenths of a Cent

A major implication of all this is that on the large volumes of gasoline involved even the smallest per gallon reduction in expenses is of major importance.

Motorists rarely notice the decimals, or *mills,* quoted on station signs and pumps. To the customer, naturally, the difference hardly seems important between, for instance, 31.9 cents and 31.5 cents.

But in such a bulk business as gasoline, a few mills mean a lot to everybody—suppliers, jobbers, dealers, and "independent marketers."

In fact the nation buys about 67 billion gallons of gasoline a year, and a single mill per gallon on this comes to about $67,000,000. Anybody in the business who can find a way to save a mill per gallon, and apply this to any appreciable volume of gasoline, can do well for himself.

And since gasoline handling expenses per gallon are greater as the trip to the customer progresses, the opportunities are greater in the later stages for economies that will have a significant impact on per gallon costs.

The layman doesn't hear much about the cost-cutting advances of the various competitors in refining and bulk transportation—fields in which several billion dollars were laid out during the 1950's and 1960's. But none of these cost-cutting advances could, in the nature of things, have as much effect on the cost of delivering a gallon of gasoline as cost-cutting changes in the local delivery and retail sale of the product.

It is important that there be no misunderstanding of what has been discussed to this point in this chapter. The discussion has been solely on the *costs* of doing business that fall upon gasoline suppliers and marketers—not the *prices* they charge. Because of the need to meet intense competition, cost is sometimes only a small consideration in establishing a gasoline price. An individual supplier or marketer might like to keep a neat and tidy relationship between his cost figures and his prices—but he seldom succeeds.

PRICE, VOLUME, AND COST

American industry in the twentieth century has had one overriding virtue—from the consumer's viewpoint. It has had a proclivity for constant experimentation with price and volume, the aim being a larger *total profit* from a smaller *unit profit*. The idea has been that lowering prices might result in large volume, which might result in lower per unit costs, which might result in larger total profits. Often it did. The big money has been made, and the big companies built, on this "mass production for the masses" principle.

This kind of experiment was dramatized by Henry Ford when he undertook to produce a car for the unheard-of low price of $500. He guessed right. His price brought a mass demand, which made possible mass production at unheard-of low cost well under this price. But this kind of price-volume-cost experimenting had been practiced for a century before 1914 by many industries, beginning with textiles and the makers of clocks and guns.

In each case there was a sharp lowering of price, and a sharp increase in sales. Sometimes profit was made— other times losses were sustained. Such experiments were risky and often didn't pay out. If they did pay out, competitors often soon crowded in with the same methods.

From this kind of financial adventuring came many phrases. One, in the 1920's, was "profitless prosperity." Later came talk of the "economics of overhead costs" (and its corollary: "spread your overhead over many production units"). Still later came the phrase "the reach for volume." This, in the gasoline business, was applied in both service-station and refinery operations.

In any case, these typically American business policies —experimenting with the possible interplay of price, volume, and costs to reach a maximum total profit—are far advanced beyond the old-fashioned and essentially naive idea of starting with an arbitrarily estimated cost, and then adding a hoped-for profit, to arrive at a hoped-for price.

The High Cost of Sitting Still

Inverse relations between volume and cost exist all through the gasoline business. But particularly at its two

35

ends—the refinery and the service station—there is a constant inducement to reach for volume. This inducement is at work even before the ground is broken for construction; the temptation is to "build for the future."

An everyday analogy may illustrate what this means. A city motorist buys a car for $3,000 and drives it a thousand miles during its first year. What are his costs? Considering depreciation, insurance, garage, etc., they can easily come to $1,000, or a dollar a mile, even though his direct operating costs—gas and oil—could scarcely amount to more than $25 of this.

But suppose he drives his car 10,000 miles. His per-mile costs now drop to perhaps 12 cents a mile, for his "fixed charges" or "overhead costs" have been spread over ten times the mileage.

And if he wants to "ram up the mileage" still further, what do the additional miles cost him? The average for *all* his miles (perhaps a dime)? Or merely his out-of-pocket costs per additional mile (perhaps two cents)?

Some Economics of Refining

A refinery is somewhat like a car. Its overhead costs go on and on whether it runs or not. It has been likened to a horse in a stable, which eats whether it works or not. When completely shut down, it is like a commercial airliner in the hangar—a huge investment earning nothing.

Well over half the costs of a refinery persist whether

36

the refinery is running at full capacity, or at half capacity, or is shut down.

Today, a refinery, like almost any manufacturing plant, can usually be run at somewhat less than capacity and produce a return that its management can live with —though, perhaps, not get rich on. But the management is often sorely tempted to increase the output beyond that point, for, with fixed costs having been recouped, the extra production entails only "running expenses." These "running expenses"—the costs of raw materials and labor—are comparable to the out-of-pocket costs to the motorist who chooses to run his car an extra 1,000 miles.

The Argument over the Incremental Barrels

The extra barrels of output have been referred to as "incremental barrels." And much controversy has come to rage in the gasoline business about them.

The question is, "How much do they really cost?" Do incremental barrels cost only raw materials and direct labor? Or do *all* barrels cost the same, with costs averaged out more and more thinly as output increases?

The choice is important because it can make so much difference in pricing outlook. Shall the refiner, for instance, price all his gasoline uniformly? If so, should he reach out for additional volume with a slightly lower uniform price level on the theory that he is coming out ahead by reducing his cost per barrel? Or should he make special lower-price sales here and there on the assumption that even though the price is low, his incremental-barrel cost on such sales is still lower?

This is no classroom exercise in dialectics. It is a daily, constant problem to gasoline refiner-suppliers.

Other Industries, Same Problem

Petroleum refining is not unique in this costing and pricing problem. The problem normally affects any industry where there are heavy investments—where overhead is an important factor in total costs. Among these industries are other forms of refining, such as metals and sugar; also the hotel business, automobile manufacturing, and printing and publishing.

In all these businesses the effect of large proportionate overhead costs appears particularly in the prices charged for what product remains after regular customers have been satisfied. Sometimes they appear as "bargain-basement sales," "publisher's overstock sales," or "high trade-in values."

Surplus or Scarcity

These problems of pricing the last barrel, book, or hotel room are of significance only when there is an excess of supply. But excess or surplus supply is *normal* in American industry and characteristic of our competitive enterprise system. This is not merely because plants are built big enough for projected future demand. It is because of the natural tendency of American business to "reach for volume."

Scarcity, in this country, is an abnormal situation.

When it occurs, it is generally caused by war or governmental action.

In time of scarcity everything is reversed—for the "last barrel" customer. The last barrel goes for a higher, not a lower, price. Cut-rate sales of everything dry up. This is a "seller's market"—in which sellers call the price tune.

But no "seller's market" appears in sight today for the gasoline business. Gasoline has been in a "buyer's market" for years, and appears likely to remain so for many years to come. Some gasoline marketers seem to think that overhanging surpluses of capacity and product are peculiar to their own business. Actually, with surpluses in many commodities, it's "tough all over." But things, perhaps, are particularly tough in the gasoline market.

Incremental Gallons—at the Service Station

In recent years, gasoline marketers have often criticized refiners for driving down the market by producing so many incremental barrels of gasoline. Refiners might well reply that this is the pot calling the kettle black. Service-station operators—be they major-brand dealers, "independent chains," or supermarkets—often have essentially the same hopes for volume (or call them temptations if you will). And their acts often lead to the same consequences.

The difference is only in method, or sequence of actions. The refiner generally runs extra barrels, at what he considers lower costs, in the hope that the cost of his product—particularly these last barrels—will go down further than the price goes down. The service-station operator, however, proceeds in reverse order. He lowers his price in the hope that this may increase his volume. Thereafter, he is like the refiner. He has the same idea in mind: to make a larger *total* profit by taking a smaller profit *per gallon* on more volume. The service-station operator, too, like the refiner, has a considerable amount of relatively fixed costs—rent, light, heat, insurance, etc. And, just as in a refinery operation, on a per-gallon basis these fixed costs thin out as volume increases.

THE CRITICS AND THE REACH
FOR VOLUME

In sum, per gallon cost in the gasoline business is *not* something inflexible, readily arrived at, which uncompromisingly determines price. Instead, it is itself strongly affected by price, acting through volume. The three—cost, price, volume—actually constitute a triangle of interrelating factors.

The gasoline business, in short, is constantly experimenting to:

1. lower *price,* so as to increase *volume;*
2. increase *volume,* so as to lower per unit *costs;* and
3. lower per unit *costs,* so as to lower *prices.*

While all this sounds like an aimless round-the-mulberry-bush race, from price to volume to cost to price, it is neither aimless nor altruistic. It is designed to increase total profits. And the gasoline business, in its treatment of *costs* as merely one of several factors of profit, is typical of progressive American business in general.

Refiners and marketers would probably take a wry attitude toward the following description by an early twentieth-century economist, Professor Thorstein Veblen, who referred to American businessmen in general as:

> unremittingly engaged in a routine of acquisition in which they habitually reach their ends by a *shrewd restriction of output.**

Some refiners and marketers and other businessmen might say, "Would we could do it!" But the nature and temperament of the American gasoline business, as one example, never seems to allow it.

* Thorstein Veblen, *The Engineers and the Price System* (New York, The Viking Press, 1921), p. 40.

CHAPTER IV

THE PRICING OF GASOLINE

> "There are more things in heaven and
> earth, Horatio,
> Than are dreamt of in your philosophy."
> *Hamlet:* Act I, Scene 5

THE GENERAL PRICE STRUCTURE

The Fabric of Gasoline Prices

The United States gasoline business has a going structure of prices. And these prices, as will be explained, relate only partially to the manufacturing and handling costs discussed in the previous chapter.

To begin with, there are the base wholesale prices of gasoline in large quantities at refineries in the key regions.

Then there is a second level of wholesale prices:

prices at terminals, before the final fan-out. These are sometimes still called tank-car prices, from the original medium of delivery out of these terminals.

The final and perhaps most important wholesale price is the tank-wagon price, from the supplier or jobber to the retail gasoline dealer, on delivery to the service station.

As to the retail price, there are, with few exceptions, no "manufacturer's retail list prices" in gasoline. The supplier's ownership of the gasoline generally ends at the service-station tanks, and the dealer is then free to set his pump at whatever retail price he chooses.

An important exception occurs when, as in New Jersey since the middle 1950's, some suppliers avail themselves of state "fair trade" laws that permit the manufacturer to set a specific retail price as the minimum to be charged for his branded product.

But major-brand suppliers by no means lose interest in the price of their gasoline when they sell it to the service-station man. The supplier's interest is natural. He wants his brand to be competitive. Most suppliers counsel with their dealers about staying competitive; but, in the absence of "fair trade" or other exceptional circumstances, the decision is strictly the dealer's.

Independent chains operate differently for the most part. Their station operators are usually on salary. They don't sell *to* the station operator, but *through* him. They don't suggest the retail price. They set it.

To a small degree, major suppliers are engaged in direct retailing, too. At a station where any supplier is itself the retailer, it, of course, establishes the price.

All the prices mentioned above—wholesale and retail —are so interrelated that they are constantly pulling each other up and down, so what is generally called a price *structure* for the gasoline business might better be called a *fabric* of prices.

Private Brand Differentials

Lesser-known brands of gasoline often sell at a price below that of better-known brands. The differential—a frequent bone of contention—may run to several cents a gallon. It is not necessarily due to a difference in quality; but often it is due to a difference in familiarity to the automobile driver or to a difference between stations in services available. Lesser-known brands range in quality from mediocre to the best. They are sometimes said to be sold "on price" while major brands are said to be sold "on reputation." However, the private brander is naturally interested in *building* a reputation. In some instances these lesser-known private brands are actually owned and promoted by major suppliers.

Bulk Sales

There is a category of gasoline sales whose prices hardly fit into the above-mentioned structure or fabric of gasoline prices at all. These are sales to large-scale buyers such as bus lines, truck fleets, highway contractors,

44

cab fleets, the federal government, states, cities, etc. In the trade, these are generally called "consumer sales," because the buyers consume the gasoline themselves; they do not resell it.

Prices on such sales are often low—sometimes below those to jobbers or dealers. Some of the reasons are obvious. These are quantity sales. Costs are low and credit risks small. No advertising or merchandising is required. And they frequently are once-in-a-while sales. There is sometimes a further reason for them—distress surplus of product. This will be discussed later.

The Living Price Structure

Gasoline prices are even more than a fabric, with flexibility and stretch. The gasoline price "structure" is a living, changing thing, to which thousands of men contribute their thinking. As a result, it is constantly responding to all kinds of changes in such things as business conditions, weather, traffic, and customers' habits and income.

LOGISTIC AND OTHER PROBLEMS

Right Time, Place, and Volume

The daily forwarding of more than 175 million gallons of gasoline from refineries by varied channels to 211,000 service stations, and from there to millions of customers, recalls what lexicographer Dr. Samuel Johnson once said of a woman preaching or of a dog walking on its hind legs: "the wonder is not that it is done well, but that it is done at all." For it is not enough merely to

45

have the supply lines. The gasoline must be dispatched to the right places, at the right time, in the right volume, all the way from the refinery.

For such movement, suppliers must prepare well in advance, clear back to the refinery. In the spring they must start increasing gasoline output for the summer months; but in the late summer they must start cutting back on gasolines to make more heating oils available for the winter.

Suppliers, however, must do more than merely try to have *enough* gasoline for expected demand at the right outlets at the right time. They must also be sure of being able to meet any unexpected additional demand. In this respect they are like fresh milk suppliers, or power companies, which must always have spare capacity on hand. Conversely, if they guess wrong and over-produce at any given time, they may find themselves with a troublesome excess of products to get rid of.

All this requires careful advance estimates of a host of diverse influences on the gasoline market. These include general business conditions and consumer buying power; population trends; changes in the public's highway travel preferences; changes in consumption of oil products in competition with other lures for the consumer dollar; and above all, the weather. And these must be worked down into the details within areas, counties, and cities.

Mistakes Are Bound to Occur

Suppliers will use anything from a small market-forecasting department to a computer to figure this all out.

46

But with competitors in all areas, of all sizes, all marketing methods, and all competitive moods, each supplier faces one more large-scale question mark: "How much of the market can we hold, or gain, in the face of constantly changing competitive conditions?"

Now let us sit in with a supplier's marketing manager, and see an unavoidable mistake about to be made. He and his company have just estimated that during the following March, three months away, they will be able to sell 5 per cent more gasoline in his area than during the *previous* March. He is making the arrangements for movement of the proper amount of gasoline to his terminals and stations.

But when March arrives, it rains and it snows. Motorists stay home by the thousands. When the month is over, they have bought 5 per cent *less* of his company's gasoline than in the previous March. And to complicate his problem—since it was cold, customers bought more heating oil than he had anticipated. Thus, he faced the headache of bringing in additional quantities of that product even though his storage facilities were already overburdened with unneeded gasoline.

Weather is the most unforeseeable force that can bring about market miscalculation. And it is a constant hazard to the refiner as well as to the marketer. The refiner may count on a cold winter and find by February that he has made too much heating oil and not enough gasoline. In the spring he may count on a good driving summer and find by August that he has made too much gasoline.

47

But other factors can also upset the best-laid plans. An aggressive competitor may take away business. Depressed prices in an adjacent area may drain away gallonage. Or the local crop may fail, or the local mills shut down.

What to Do with the Surplus?

Our unlucky supplier now has excess gasoline on his hands. What shall he do about it?

He has three choices—basically those available to all sellers in the gasoline business when they find themselves with extra gasoline.

He can:

1. store the excess gasoline;
2. dispose of it through regular marketing channels; or
3. find a fast outlet.

Now let us consider his choices. For this is essentially a typical situation. It is a dramatization of the general problems involved in gasoline pricing.

The Costs of Storage

Let us now suppose that our marketing manager with excess gasoline on hand decides to hold it in storage until he can gradually work it off.

It isn't a very satisfactory choice.

To begin with, gasoline storage is expensive in relation to gasoline's price, which essentially can be kept low only by a timely flow to market. Stoppage in the movement of

48

gasoline immediately begins to cost. For storage costs money.

But far more serious than the storage cost is the backup effect. New product cannot be delivered to terminals until there is room for it. If storage space is short, refinery output may have to be cut back. The effect can be felt clear back to the oil field. If the refiner is part of a crude-oil-producing company, then the company's crude-oil output may have to be cut. If the refiner gets his crude from outside his own company, he may run the risk of losing some of his regular crude-oil sources.

So the flow of gasoline may be compared to a river. If too much comes down the river, then the excess must be drained off into reservoirs or it will break the levee somewhere.

If, for instance, the refinery has already scheduled full runs for April, and now its outlet in our marketing manager's area is reduced by the carry-over stored from March, it may be decided to run full anyway. But where to sell the extra? It will probably go either into the "spot market," as "distress gasoline," or be sold to another refiner who has a market for the product. The pressure is now off our marketing manager—but not off his company. No doubt the extra gasoline will show up somewhere in the business, and result in a downward pressure on prices. But it probably won't show up in his area.

Thus time is forever pressuring the supplier. Not only is gasoline costly to store, but the equipment to produce and move it is expensive to keep idle. In some supply-demand situations he may have to throw original cost estimates to the wind and consider primarily the cost of *not* selling promptly.

Disposing of Gasoline through Regular Channels

Now let us suppose our marketer elects to take the second way out of his gasoline surplus—that is, to dispose of it through regular trade channels.

Apart from marketing gimmicks—special promotions, flying flags, prizes and giveaways—there is only one way to do this, and that is to cut the price.

Unhappily, however, one of the most notable things about gasoline is that demand is relatively constant.

The gasoline market is not like the market for television sets, stereo recordings, fresh strawberries, or trips to Europe, where a 50 per cent price cut can bring in large numbers of new, additional customers—or induce existing customers to increase their buying substantially.

This is not to say that motorists don't read price signs. Some are highly price-conscious, look for cut-rate stations, and will converge on depressed price areas.

But in doing this, they do not increase their total purchases. They merely switch them from one station, or area, to another. They do not appreciably drive any farther, nor burn any more gasoline. Even the most drastic price wars do not increase *total* mileage in the affected areas.

This is called short-term "inelastic demand"—demand that does not stretch and expand with lower prices.

It is quite different with gasoline's long-term demand, over years and decades. If the product weren't so reasonably priced and conveniently available, people wouldn't take so many trips nor even buy so many cars—as the European experience with extremely high-taxed, and so extremely high-priced gasoline has shown.

But it is a fact, unhappily, that a marketer's customers won't immediately increase their driving even when the price of gasoline is cut sharply. So if the marketer cuts his price, the only added sales he can make are sales to his competitors' customers.

And his competitors know this as well as he.

They can match his price—and more than likely will do so if they suspect that his lowered tank-wagon price is merely an effort to shrug off an overload of gasoline at their expense. In fact some of them may have made the same miscalculation of demand and have the same surplus problem.

So by trying the price route out of his current inventory trouble, our marketer may, in effect, do a Samson and pull down the whole area price structure around his own ears.

Finding a Fast Outlet

For our manager and his company, there is a third and final choice of how to dispose of the excess gasoline caused by weather. It is to find an outside, non-regular market and there to sell the gasoline for whatever it will bring.

The most notable of such outlets is sale on the open

market—to brokers, "independent marketers," or other large buyers. Often such sales are in hundreds of thousands of gallons and sometimes they are made on sealed bids.

To turn to such a third selling choice, our supplier must take a deep breath and remind himself of the disadvantages of the two other courses.

As was mentioned earlier, such sales are often at low prices. But they are somewhat offset by comparatively low costs (due to quantity, credit, and other economies).

Sales under distress conditions are usually at prices lower than normal bulk sale prices. The basic reasons for such often-profitless sales have been implied above. The supplier presumably has more gasoline on his hands than he wants to try pushing into regular channels, or storing. He has been "caught long." And as a result he is, in his own interest and after careful calculation, acting to avoid what might possibly be a very great loss under one of the other two alternatives.

LOSS TODAY; PROFIT (?) TOMORROW

In some circumstances, for good and sufficient though temporary reasons, a refiner may be willing to produce and sell gasoline at prices well below the most optimistic estimate of last-barrel cost.

The start of this dismal story may be when he finds he must lower his price to a certain level in order to hold his own against competition, and his accountants tell him that, at that price, "no matter *how* we figure it," there will be a loss on every barrel of output.

His natural first thought would be to curtail production or even to shut down.

But neither will save him much money. His fixed costs will keep on.

So it may be more economical to keep running and lose only a *little* money every day, rather than to slow down or shut down and lose *even more* money every day.

Besides, our refiner wouldn't want to add to his other troubles the substantial costs of refinery shut-down and start-up, nor the disruptions of laying off labor, dropping crude-oil "connections" (sources of crude oil), and cutting off regular jobbers and dealers.

So he keeps refining, selling for whatever he can get, and hoping that the market may soon recover.

A marketer can find himself in a situation analogous to that of our refiner. He can find himself in a depressed market that he feels is only temporarily so. Assuming things will get better and knowing that he may lose his established marketing position if he closes up, he keeps operating in the area even though it may mean months without profit.

There is at least one other circumstance in which a gasoline refiner or marketer may for a time sell at a profitless price or even, where it is legal, at a price below the lowest possible estimate of his particular costs.

The circumstance might occur when he tries to break

into a new market that to him looks lucrative for the future. As a new entrant in the market his costs are probably high for he lacks the local facilities necessary for efficient operation; yet he sets his price low to attract customers. He may figure that he will have to forego profits for a time, in the hope of getting established and making money later. Some economists would regard such losses as an investment.

"Predatory" Pricing

One form of taking business losses for future profit is only a historical memory: selling below cost in a particular area in the specific hope of ruining a weak or small competitor and then taking over his business and his customers. This, called a "predatory practice," was fairly common in the old days when the oil business was young and uncrowded. It is illegal now, but even if it were not there would be very little chance in the gasoline business of so calling one's competitive shots today. In any market there are too many eager competitors, major and minor, branded and unbranded—all ready to fight to preserve their own positions, and ready, too, to move into any market vacuum created by the demise of one in their ranks. Today, anybody in the gasoline business foolhardy enough to wage a predatory campaign would find its successful completion no simple matter.

In this age of gasoline marketing, a firm's moving into a new area does not forebode less competition. It means more of it.

The Profit Is the Pay-off

Whether sellers taking a loss on a sale do so to avoid a greater loss, or to gain a future profit, it is a sometimes forgotten truism that profit is inevitably the ultimate motive.

While in the short run price must both meet competition and move the goods, in the long run it must more than cover costs. It is a certainty that no one can afford to handle gasoline in any branch of the business at a loss, knowingly *and continuously*.

In sound, profit-seeking business practice, every type of sale and every offering price must justify itself either by contributing to a profit, immediate or eventual, or by minimizing a loss.

SOME PREMISES OF GASOLINE PRICING

The Protean Values of Gasoline

The value of a bulky commodity like gasoline varies "all over the place." Gasoline of the same specifications may be worth so much today, more tomorrow, and less the next day; so much here, and more there, or vice versa. Gasoline is not like diamonds or gold, the value of which varies little from San Francisco to London or from this year to next year. Its value is more like the value of such bulky staples as firewood, which may cost $20 a cord in New England near the woods, and 50 cents a stick in New York City. Perhaps the best analogy is with water —worth less than nothing in flood, but worth a great deal in the desert.

The Flexibility of Gasoline Prices

Due to the almost infinite variety of circumstances in which gasoline finds itself from market to market and from time to time, it is hard to figure any fixed formulas for pricing it.

Yet there is always the imperative profit-seeking command that prices must be arrived at that will move the goods most economically to wherever they are most wanted at the moment.

Gasoline prices are never in equilibrium with all the supply-and-demand forces that affect them. They are chronically in need of adjustment. Pricing decisions must be made without delay. These decisions may be wrong half the time. (If they are wrong too often the maker leaves the scene.) But they have to be made by those closest to the circumstances. To learn *everything* about the hows and whys of gasoline pricing at any particular moment, you would have to talk with about everybody in the business.

The Art of Guessing Right Prices

The quoting or bidding of gasoline prices cannot be a science. It has to be a day-to-day art—a matter of trial-and-error dependent basically on judgment. The factors that go into the pricing of gasoline will always be hard to figure. Prices are always experimental.

On the supply side, the seller must figure on costs that are arguable to start with and that may vary inversely with a volume that is unpredictable. And on the demand side, he faces changing weather, business conditions, and *competition*. Overall estimates of national consumption can tell him lamentably little about the next few months in City X, County Y, or State Z.

The gasoline marketer has no slide rule to tell him how far, in a good market, he can afford to expand; nor how far, in a poor market, he can figure to keep selling at a loss to avoid a greater loss.

This is what has given the business, through its price system, its remarkable flexibility, pliability, challenge, and life.

CHAPTER V

GASOLINE PRICE WARS

WHAT, WHERE, WHEN?

How They Start

The gasoline business in the city of X is quiet. It seems a rather routine business. Nothing much is happening except that customers are buying perhaps 100,000 gallons a day from the city's 75 stations.

Most major-brand stations on the main thoroughfares are selling gasoline at 32.9 cents (including tax). Major brands less popular in the area are selling at 31.9 cents. Stations selling "independent" brands are posting 30.9 cents. These differentials—of which the dealers are far more conscious than most motorists—have stood for weeks, or perhaps months. Prices seem frozen.

On side streets, however, and in residential areas, the motorist may find a good deal of price variety. At some stations he will find a higher price, but better service. Or he may have a favorite station, because he likes the dealer, and here he doesn't even notice what the price is. Or he may be very price-conscious and have found a cut-price station. There he gets no service such as windshield wiping, checking the oil and tires, etc.; but these things, he figures, he can do very well for himself.

By and large, everything seems static in the city. Nothing is happening. All 75 varied price signs of perhaps 20 brands are in a state of peaceful coexistence.

Then something happens. Perhaps one of the 32.9-cent signs comes down and is changed to 31.9 cents. Or one of the 30.9-cent signs is changed to 29.9 cents. Or a 29.9-cent sign becomes 27.9 cents.

Competitors notice it first. And for a time they choose to ignore it. Price tranquillity is an apple-cart that almost everybody is loath to upset. And if motorists don't notice the cut, the price-cutter "gets away with it"—but his only result is to lose money.

However, motorists may begin to notice it and switch to the price-cutting dealer. Or if they don't, he may set large price signs by the curb, cut another cent, and fly banners and streamers to attract attention. If this dealer finally begins to pull in business from other stations, a price war may be on.

Not all price wars start precisely this way. Each begins differently. The provocations, incidents, and opening gambits are of great variety. The "unpleasantness" may have started with the quiet changing of price signs for several weeks before the war was openly on. In contrast it may have been begun by somebody—perhaps a newcomer—with all flags flying and offering premium baits and giveaways, such as toys, picnic equipment, glassware, trips, cars, and trading stamps.

Nor is there any uniformity in the kind of station at which price wars start. They may begin with major-brand stations, or "independent" marketers' stations. In fact one price war in the early 1960's is said to have started when a single operator of a portable "skid station" cut his price far below the prices of local "independents." Major-brand dealers at first ignored him, but the lower-priced "independents" cut to cope with him, then the higher-priced "independents" to cope with them, then the semi-majors, and finally the major-brand stations started to come in, until the whole local price structure went down like a row of dominoes.

Often, however, nobody can agree on just how, where, or with whom a fracas started.

Where to Find a Price War

At almost any time in the early 1960's, dozens of gasoline price wars, small or large, short or prolonged, were raging in the United States.

They were epidemic in the business and chronic in many cities. In fact they were so widespread across the country as to defy characterization. They occurred in small towns and large cities; sometimes they extended scores of miles along well-traveled routes; and they broke out both near to and far from sources of supply.

The gasoline business in Chicago was down with a price war all through the summer of 1962, and price wars flared again in 1963 and early 1964. Gasoline markets in the larger coastal cities of Texas were upset by price wars in the spring of 1963. So were Oklahoma markets. And at any given time in recent years, so have gasoline markets in a dozen medium-sized cities from coast to coast.

Sometimes one gasoline war succeeded another in the same area, until they seemed commonplace. Over a 15-year period in the Los Angeles area, price wars were so frequent as sometimes to seem the normal thing—with interspersed periods of "normal" prices appearing to be the *abnormal* thing. In Detroit price-war conditions remained so constant through several years, including 1964, that it was dubbed within the industry as "the worst market in the country."

Price wars may start in areas where new highways have taken away traffic and the sidetracked dealers begin to fight for what is left.

In contrast, such price competition may also start in areas of great traffic promise, where everybody is building for a big future—which has not yet arrived.

How Wide, How Deep, and How Long?

Price wars can be measured three ways: by how far they spread; by how deeply the prices are slashed; and by how long the war lasts. And in none of these dimensions do they have any particular standards or boundaries.

Breadth. A price war may involve only a handful of stations in a neighborhood or along one local strip of highway. But some wars have rippled out to a radius of 100 miles, stopping only at a natural boundary—a wide-open space or a river, for instance.

Depth. Price wars have driven retail gasoline prices down so far as to wipe out the equivalent of the dealer's entire margin and a considerable part of the supplier's tank-wagon price. There is no telling in advance how far the contestants will go in their price cuts.

Duration. Nor do price wars have any predictable length of life. They may last for a week, for six months, or, intermittently, for years.

Like bad weather, price wars always end. Somebody decides to see if he can cut his losses or move his prices back to a profitable level. By then other competitors may be equally fed up with sub-normal prices, and the whole market may recover.

But if others do not follow, the stations pricing more normally will soon be forced back down, and the price war will continue.

THE SUPPLIER'S ROLE IN A PRICE WAR
The Retailer in Trouble

When posted retail prices start tumbling, it is the dealer who first feels the brunt of the cuts if he chooses to match them. If his margin is five cents, then even a one-cent drop could mean he is taking a 20 per cent cut in his income from gasoline; by the time the cuts reach a nickel, he could be pumping gasoline for love; and if the competitive price cuts go below that, he could find himself selling gasoline to the public for less than he is paying for it. But the burden in any case is usually lightened by the supplier.

The retailer, more often than not, appeals to his supplier for relief, and he usually gets it. That is, he gets a lower tank-wagon price to enable him to stay in business without rapidly going broke.

The Supplier's Problem

The supplier most often feels that he must sell at a competitive price. If he doesn't, he might lose his dealers; and good dealers are scarce. The supplier always needs well-manned outlets. So he comes to the dealer's financial aid.

He rarely does this by directly cutting the tank-wagon price. Instead he grants the embattled dealer a "voluntary competitive price allowance" off the tank-wagon price. Sometimes this is called simply a subsidy.

Suppliers have all kinds of policies in granting these allowances. They range from the austere to the liberal. The supplier himself is in a spot. He doesn't want to be too hard on the retailer, or he will lose him. He doesn't want to be too easy, or the retailer may happily keep on cutting prices, almost entirely at the supplier's expense. He doesn't want to be too hasty, either, for he doesn't want to be the only supplier giving an allowance. Thus he waits to be sure that competing suppliers have reduced *their* prices to dealers as well.

A supplier seldom takes the entire burden of a price

reduction on himself. He takes part of it. The dealer, therefore, has an incentive to return his price to normal at the first opportunity.

Under some suppliers' plans the supplier shares the dealer's shrinkage of margin on a graduated scale; under others the supplier shares a percentage of the dealer's loss of margin. Under a typical plan, the supplier absorbs 75 or 80 per cent of the drop in price, and the dealer absorbs the rest. A few plans call for the supplier and dealer to split the burden fifty-fifty.

Jobbers usually also get price-war support along some of the lines suggested above. This is logical. The jobber also supplies embattled retailers. He is supposed to pass the allowance on to them. And under most plans he, too, shares part of the price cut. He contributes to the allowance, in part, out of his own pocket.

Many suppliers, however, go further. They give their dealers and jobbers a "minimum margin guarantee" or *"stop-out."* This means that no matter how deep the price war may drive prices, the dealers and jobbers are still guaranteed so-and-so-much gross margin, or markup, on each gallon sold. In severe price wars such minimum guarantees are extremely costly to suppliers.

"Wide-Area Pricing"

Gasoline price wars, by nature, tend to spread. This can be costly to suppliers operating over a wide area.

So besides the problems of how *much* to support dealers and how *long* to do so, the supplier has the problem of how *widely* to do so.

The supplier has every incentive to localize the price

war. However, price wars tend to pull demand into price-depressed areas, drain it from neighboring areas, and so to pull down going price structures over wider and wider areas.

In recent years a few of the larger suppliers have experimented with "wide-area" or "large-area" pricing. As a policy, they keep their tank-wagon prices the same over large geographic areas, in some cases over half a state. Thus the price charged by one of these suppliers is the same in neighboring areas. Wide-area pricing, of course, means an immediate widespread price cut, if a cut should come. But advocates of the plan say that, in the long run, this is less disruptive. As a concomitant, these same suppliers have tried to discourage price wars by keeping their "normal" prices at levels they feel to be "realistically low"; and they try to resist giving subsidies if price wars do, nevertheless, break out.

But this kind of supplier effort to resist temptation, and to be stony-hearted toward embattled dealers, has its limits and handicaps. There are those who say that these suppliers' dealers suffer margin cuts in price wars that make it hard for them to survive, and that the plan itself inevitably brings about the spread of a price war that might otherwise be contained.

SOME CAUSES OF PRICE WARS
Tempers and Criticisms

Price wars, naturally, hurt everybody involved in the business—dealers, jobbers, suppliers, and "independent marketers," as well as their employees. In effect, nobody in the trade ever "wins" a price war. Often even the motorist doesn't win; hard-pressed dealers have to let expected services slide.

In the trade an assured outcome of a price war is the rising of tempers. Everybody in the business is accused, and perhaps rightly, of having either caused or unnecessarily contributed to the war. The invidious term "price cutter" is bandied about, but usually without much real certainty as to who this is. As the *Oil & Gas Journal* once put it, rather facetiously, in its "Journally Speaking" column:

> we have been making a little investigation . . . to find the price-cutter . . . the bad boy who starts price wars. . . .
>
> In gasoline price wars the bad guys are the guys who cut the price, and the good guys are the posse . . . deputized to uphold order and decency.
>
> They all do a lot of shooting at each other with similar weapons (price cuts) to the great entertainment of the viewers (motorists) . . . all of which would be strictly according to Hoyle if only we could tell who shot first, who shot in self-defense, (and) who's against whom. . . .

Some Obvious Causes of Price Wars

Some of the immediate causes of price wars are easily recognized.

One is the frequently substantial price spread between major brands and "independent" brands of gasoline. Many marketers point out that today there is little reason for such price spreads. In the 1920's and 1930's many of the cut-rate local brands were of inferior quality and dispensed without service at bare-bones facilities. But this isn't so today. Many "independent" chains now sell top-quality gasoline at attractive stations with as much service as that offered at the best major-brand stations. Faced with such competition, a dealer selling a major brand may very well feel that he must narrow the spread. But in doing this, he may start a price war.

A price war can start the other way around, too. An "independent marketer" may seek to widen the spread. Or a conflict may start over some move to change the going differentials among the "independents" themselves.

The fact is that nobody knows how much more a motorist will pay for a familiar brand over an unfamiliar brand; but somebody in the business is constantly experimenting to find out—and sometimes the experiments touch off a price war.

Sometimes the disturbance in the spread between going prices of different brands, however, may be the surface evidence of something deeper—for instance, the invasion of an area by a locally unfamiliar brand, or the introduction by an established marketer of a new grade of product, or the expansion of an ambitious "independent" chain marketer.

Basically, price wars are started by sellers—little, intermediate, or big—who believe they have some advantage, innovation, improvement, or low-cost supply source that will enable them to come out ahead.

Practically all the competitors who are charged with starting, continuing, or aggravating price wars have one purpose in common.

They are trying to reach profit through volume—at either the refinery or the service-station end of the business.

And in doing so, they are seeking answers to questions such as these (discussed in previous chapters) :

What does the last barrel of gasoline cost at the refinery, or the last gallon at the service station? In other words, how shall costs in an industry of heavy investment be allocated?

How sensitive are customers to competitive price cuts?

How far can competitors afford to go, and for how long, to meet such price cuts?

Unfortunately for the business, price wars are for the most part the spectacular outcome of sharp competition in a high-volume industry. Of thousands of participants, each has the constant temptation to try for an immediate larger share of that volume—and for the lower per-unit costs that would go with it.

CHAPTER VI

REGULATING THE
MARKET PLACE

PRESENT LAWS

The gasoline business is chronically subject to more proposals for legal reform than perhaps any other business
in the country.

This may be because gasoline marketing is such a large
business, providing an important staple of American life
direct to the consumer. And at least partly it is a result
of the fact that there are usually some among the thousands in the oil business who are tempted to try to protect
themselves from the effects of competition through proposals for new laws.

However, there are already a good many laws on
the books that affect the business. Most are of a general

nature and affect all businesses alike, not just the oil industry.

State Laws

Many states have "one-price" and "below-cost" laws, which apply to business in general, including gasoline marketing. A few states have adopted similar laws relating particularly to petroleum products.

A typical "one-price" law says in effect that a product may be sold at only one price throughout the state, except for differences due to such factors as grade, quantity, and transportation costs.

A "below-cost" law says that a product may not be sold below cost—at least where there is intent to injure competition.

These laws were written to cope with a situation that existed in the late nineteenth century, when this type of legislation came into vogue. This was the era when the present major staple industries were starting. In many industries it was the practice for a leading supplier to try to monopolize the business by lowering its prices wherever it ran into opposition, and then holding them down until the weaker local competitor either failed or had to join the monopoly.

Note that this was for the direct and obvious purpose of injuring a particular competitor, and so with the intent of preventing or eliminating competition.

Feeling ran high near the turn of the century, particularly in the farm states, against this kind of price manipulation and its practitioners. And so it was essentially against this type of practice that the first state "one-price" and "below-cost" laws were written.

Federal Laws

The Sherman Antitrust Act, passed by Congress in 1890, has so much prestige and is so widely known that —figuratively speaking—it has just about become a part of the United States Constitution.

Its first two sections contain its prohibitions. Section 1 forbids combinations in restraint of trade; and the courts long ago interpreted this to include, among other things, "price-fixing"—any kind of joint efforts to hold prices either up, down, or steady. Section 2 prohibits not only monopolies, but also attempts at monopoly.

In 1914 President Wilson and Congress felt that further federal legislation was needed, specifically aimed at "predatory practices" and "unfair trade practices." Two laws were passed.

The Federal Trade Commission Act of September 26, 1914, declared "unfair methods of competition in commerce" to be unlawful. And it created the Federal Trade Commission to administer this law.

The Clayton Act of October 15, 1914, among other things, made it unlawful "to discriminate in price between different purchasers . . . where the effect . . . may be to substantially lessen competition or tend to create a monopoly. . . ." But the Act allowed differences in price on account of differences in grade, quality, or quantity, or in the cost of selling or transport, or "made in good faith to meet competition."

The Spirit of These Laws

The broad intent of these laws, both state and federal, was to make competition more intense and strenuous. President Wilson in 1914 said he would take off his hat to the man who, by selling more at lower prices and by improving the quality of his product, could take business away from his competitors.

The writers of these laws assumed that in business competition somebody was bound to get hurt. They merely aimed to set up some Marquis of Queensberry rules to prevent the use of practices deemed likely to lessen competition and thereby to hurt the consumer.

The "Great Divide" in the Antitrust Laws

The Clayton Act was drastically amended by the Robinson-Patman Anti-Price Discrimination Act of 1936. This law tightened considerably the "anti-price discrimination" provisions of the Clayton Act. It also made selling at "unreasonably low prices" a criminal offense. Some have considered this law the federal equivalent of the state "one-price" and "below-cost" statutes. But in the price discrimination field it goes much further and has had far more impact on business.

The Robinson-Patman Act, in spirit, marked a reversal of the American antitrust tradition of hard competition. The Act itself was born soon after a major breach in the antitrust laws: the National Industrial Recovery Act of 1933, which set aside the Sherman Act to let businessmen

72

and labor unions work out agreements to raise prices and wages.

The principal effect of the Robinson-Patman Act is to narrow the circumstances under which it is legal to charge a lower price to one customer than to another—or, in the words of the law, to "discriminate in price." It defies a very fundamental competitive concept: price competition to win business.

The gasoline business is, by its nature, inextricably involved in the interpretations of this law. For so widely do gasoline values vary, in time and place, that the first law of gasoline pricing is flexibility, and this often unavoidably means different prices for the same product at different times, places, or circumstances. Yet, in the terms of the Robinson-Patman Act, this may spell "discrimination" against someone, somewhere. Unless specifically permitted in the law (as interpreted), "discrimination" can be a troublesome legal word to run afoul of.

PROBLEMS OF REGULATION

The Obscurity of the Law

Courts, lawyers, and marketers have seemingly endless difficulties interpreting the Robinson-Patman Act.

The key section of this measure, 2a, is a single sentence of 347 words, punctuated by four important "Provided's."

The meaning of some parts of Section 2 of the law sometimes takes years to find out. Section 2b, relating to the right to meet a competitor's price in good faith, is particularly obscure. One Section 2b case, arising from wholesale gasoline prices in Detroit, was in and out of the Federal Trade Commission and the courts for eighteen years. Many questions about the Act have never been settled, even after nearly thirty years of much litigation and many court opinions. A Supreme Court Justice in 1963 called the Act "a singularly opaque and elusive statute" in ruling on a gasoline case involving a price war and the question of how far suppliers might grant subsidies to dealers.

As was said in *Oil Prices and Competition* (Fleming, 1953):

> Suppliers differ in how far and how widely they will share their dealers' price-war difficulties. For price-cutting can easily spread from a city to a county and from there up and down a main highway.
>
> If local dealers get help, the next outer circle of dealers want it too, and then the next. This presents difficulties. Supplying companies have to bear in mind the prohibitions in the Clayton and Robinson-Patman Acts against discrimination between one customer (dealer) and another one next door or a mile down the highway but in the same trading area.
>
> And the definition of *trading area* depends on what law department you consult.

At the time this current book was being written, despite years of hearings in scores of law cases, the answers to the questions that these problems raise were still not settled by the courts. Instead of answers there were even more questions, more uncertainties.

The supplier has an economic and a legal problem. No matter how narrowly or broadly he draws the geographical line on price-war "voluntary competitive allowances," he still faces the legal risk that he may be accused of "price discrimination" against his other dealers outside this line.

It was suggested by the Supreme Court in 1963 that the supplier might meet the problem of fairness to his dealers in and around a price-war vortex by "feathering out" or graduating his allowances. However, the court did not fully endorse this procedure or set forth any guidelines as to how it could be put into practice in specific cases. Such a pricing schedule would still be subject to legal challenge. It could even invite litigation by increasing the range and importance of a price war.

The Complexity of the Law

The Sherman Antitrust Act of 1890 in its leading sections (Section 1 against conspiracy and Section 2 against monopoly) is brief, like a Constitutional article.

But with the Clayton Act, complexities entered the law. It had to include "provided's" and "however's." This was because the Clayton Act embodied principles too broad for unmitigated application to the complexities of business. A flat "one-price" requirement, or a flat "below-cost" ban on pricing, for instance, would immediately put any business in a bind. So the writers of this law put in a series of necessary exceptions. Prices could legally be lower, for instance, in cases of quantity discounts, or to reflect differences in selling or transportation costs, or to reflect differences in grade or quality. And then the Clayton Act writers put in a further exception: the "good faith" provision that a seller could cut prices for *some* customers, below others, to meet competition. They also limited the ban on price "discrimination" to "where the effect . . . may be to substantially lessen competition or tend to create a monopoly."

And when the Robinson-Patman Act sharpened the sword of the law, still more provisos and qualifications had to be included lest the law bind business too tightly and cause the flexibility of free pricing to vanish.

Since then, many proposals to further tighten the laws, particularly those applying to the gasoline business, have been held back or discouraged because of the possible "side effects." For complex new laws may prove to have unexpected consequences unwanted by the authors.

State Regulation Proposals

Meantime, in more than one state capital, bills have been proposed to put the gasoline business in the state under the equivalent of a public utility commission that would have the last say on such things as prices, profits, margins, and station building.

The plan, as usually presented, is even more ambitious than federal regulation, since it proposes a public utility status for the business. Normally, public utilities have exclusive franchises, or monopolies, in their areas. "No

Trespass" signs are put up against would-be competitors. It is in exchange for this that the state steps in to regulate the prices of such utilities; the state may even dictate where service must be provided. But the state regulatory commission is supposed to allow companies so regulated prices that will yield a "fair return" on investment.

All this is quite different from regulating a wide-open competitive business such as gasoline. Nobody in the gasoline business has any shield against competition or any guarantee of "fair return" on investment. To put such a business under the double pressure of both free, wide-open competition and of regulation would be unreasonable. To treat it as a monopoly would probably tend to *make* it a monopoly—with insiders kept in and outsiders kept out.

Another pitfall for state regulation lies in the natural competition between the states. In every state drivers benefit greatly from the intense competition in the gasoline business brought about by expanding majors, aggressive "independents," and ambitious jobbers and retailers. Regulation, as usually proposed, might easily sidetrack this benefit within a regulating state.

The only relevant experience with utility-type regulation of the gasoline business has been in two Canadian provinces, British Columbia (1934–1951) and Nova Scotia (1933–1950). In both provinces the experience was unsatisfactory—investment fell off, service deteriorated, price competition ended—and the idea was abandoned.

CHAPTER VII

CONCLUSION

Gasoline marketing—like most selling in the United States—is rough, tough, and hazardous. It has little more compassion than a poker game. It has grown on the principle, "Let the best man win!" Its most conspicuous characteristic has been its competition.

The gasoline business is *bound* to be competitive. Here are two reasons: first, the freedom with which people can enter it, price their gasoline, and use different selling methods; and second, the ability of the buyer, the motorist, to easily examine the market in the course of his normal travels.

The handling of gasoline is not just one big business. It is many businesses, involving many functions, in many areas. And into each outsiders may enter, risk their money, and price their services at any level they choose. This means not only "little fellows," for whom there are ample opportunities, but also "big fellows" who want to try selling where the grass looks greener. As in most businesses in this country, there are no preserves, no restricted areas, and no legal monopolies on function, area, or method.

Just as this freedom has naturally led to intense competition, so this competition has in turn had conspicuous natural results. These have been constant change and innovation. Nothing in the gasoline business has long remained stationary—neither structure, methods, products, nor prices. And, given the same degree of competition, the business is likely to keep on changing—as much in the next decade as in prior ones. It cannot stay the same.

Competitive change brings unending benefits for the customer in such forms as better gasoline, better services, and lower prices in relation to wages and other prices.

But competitive change also has its obverse side for existing participants in the business. The normal course of innovation is one of "creative destruction" of conventional values and methods, of competitive positions, and even of jobs.

It is here suggested that the soundest basis for judging any such business as gasoline is the degree of freedom with which energetic individuals and firms may enter the business—any part of it—and pioneer in pricing and market innovations.

So long as the gasoline business continues to spell opportunity for aggressive, imaginative, and hard-working men, it will continue to be a good business for both participants and customers.

APPENDIX TABLES

TABLE I

NUMBER AND CAPACITY OF OPERATING REFINERIES, BY REFINERY DISTRICTS

U. S. Bureau of Mines Refinery Districts	Number of Operating Refineries (1)	Operating Capacity (1) (B/D)	Crude Oil Runs to Stills (2) (B/D)
East Coast	21	1,327,400	1,106,404
Appalachian No. 1	13	121,240	105,775
Appalachian No. 2	3	118,000	101,735
Indiana, Illinois, Kentucky	48	1,763,890	1,578,437
Minnesota, Wisconsin, North and South Dakota	7	176,500	146,710
Oklahoma, Kansas, Missouri	27	820,480	743,849
Texas Inland	25	376,165	316,177
Texas Gulf Coast	26	2,355,850	2,137,437
Louisiana Gulf Coast	10	939,250	853,379
Arkansas, Louisiana Inland	17	152,450	123,076
New Mexico	7	34,475	29,538
Rocky Mountain	28	385,050	319,259
West Coast	41	1,590,521	1,295,136
Total U. S.	273	10,161,271	8,857,000

(1) *As of January 1, 1965.*
(2) *Daily average for the 1964 calendar year.*
Source: U. S. Bureau of Mines.

TABLE II

YIELD FROM A BARREL OF CRUDE OIL
1920 Vs. 1964

	1920		1964	
	Gallons Per Barrel	Per Cent Yield	Gallons Per Barrel	Per Cent Yield
Gasoline	11.0	26.1%	19.0	45.3%
Kerosine	5.3	12.7%	2.1	5.1%
Gas, Oil & Distillates ⎫			9.5	22.7%
Residual Fuel Oil ⎬	20.4	48.6%	3.4	8.2%
Other Products & Losses	5.3	12.6%	8.0	18.7%
Total	42.0	100.0%	42.0	100.0%

Source: U. S. Bureau of Mines.

TABLE III

TOTAL PETROLEUM PRODUCTS TRANSPORTED IN THE UNITED STATES, BY METHOD OF TRANSPORTATION, 1963

	Barrels Carried	Per Cent of Total
Pipelines	930,162,071	20.2%
Water Carriers	1,737,968,771	37.7%
Trucks	1,673,798,018	36.3%
Railroads	266,401,705	5.8%
Total	4,608,330,565	100.0%

Source: Association of Oil Pipe Lines and American Petroleum Institute.

TABLE IV

REFINERY PRICE OF REGULAR GRADE GASOLINE IN THE UNITED STATES 1935-1964

(Cents Per Gallon)

Year		Year	
1964	11.27¢	1949	10.71¢
1963	11.35	1948	10.53
1962	11.52	1947	8.57
1961	11.62	1946	6.60
1960	11.61	1945	6.48
1959	11.64	1944	6.47
1958	11.74	1943	6.32
1957	12.34	1942	6.14
1956	11.75	1941	6.05
1955	11.62	1940	5.26
1954	11.66	1939	5.79
1953	12.01	1938	5.97
1952	11.38	1937	6.68
1951	11.40	1936	6.32
1950	10.86	1935	5.42

Source: Independent Petroleum Association of America—refined products prices in 9 refinery markets. All prices based on low quotations from Platt's Oilgram Price Service. Individual prices weighted as follows: Okla. (16%), Midwestern Group 3 (20%), Western Penna. (5.6%), N. Y. Harbor (10.4%), Phila. (3.2%), Jacksonville (1.6%), Boston (1.6%), Gulf Coast (21.6%), & Los Angeles (20%).

TABLE V

TANK WAGON PRICE OF GASOLINE (EX. TAX) COMPARED TO CHANGES IN THE WHOLESALE PRICE INDEX AND SELECTED COMMODITIES

(1957-1959 = 100)

Year	Wholesale Price Index, All Commodities (1)	Gasoline	Rubber and Rubber Products	Pulp, Paper & Allied Products	Metals & Metal Products	Machinery & Motive Products
1964	101.2	90.8	92.5	99.0	102.8	102.9
1963	100.7	93.2	93.8	99.2	100.1	102.2
1962	100.8	94.6	93.3	100.0	100.0	102.3
1961	100.8	96.8	96.1	98.8	100.7	102.3
1960	101.3	98.5	99.9	101.8	101.3	102.4
1959	101.3	98.5	99.7	101.0	101.2	102.2
1958	99.5	99.3	100.1	100.1	99.1	100.1
1957	99.2	102.2	100.2	99.0	99.7	97.7
1956	96.5	99.9	100.6	97.2	97.8	92.1
1955	92.4	99.1	99.2	91.1	90.0	85.8
Per Cent Change 1964 over 1955	+9.5%	−8.4%	−6.8%	+8.6%	+14.2%	+20.0%

(1) Excluding Farm and Food Products.

Sources: Tank wagon price index for gasoline computed from average prices as reported by the Texas Company through June 1956 and by Platt's Oilgram Price Service for the subsequent period; other wholesale price indexes from U. S. Department of Labor, Bureau of Labor Statistics.

TABLE VI

SERVICE STATION PRICE OF GASOLINE (EX. TAX) COMPARED TO CHANGES IN THE CONSUMER PRICE INDEX AND MAJOR CONSUMER ITEMS

(1957-1959 = 100)

Year	Consumer Price Index, All Items	Gasoline	Food	Housing	Apparel	Medical Care
1964	108.1	92.5	106.4	107.2	105.7	119.4
1963	106.7	93.2	105.1	106.0	104.8	117.0
1962	105.4	94.3	103.6	104.8	103.6	114.2
1961	104.2	95.1	102.6	103.9	103.0	111.3
1960	103.1	97.2	101.4	103.1	102.2	108.1
1959	101.5	98.1	100.3	101.3	100.7	104.4
1958	100.7	99.5	101.9	100.2	99.8	100.1
1957	98.0	102.4	97.8	98.5	99.7	95.5
1956	94.7	99.9	94.7	95.5	98.4	91.8
1955	93.3	99.2	94.0	94.1	95.9	88.6
Per Cent Change 1964 over 1955	+15.9%	−6.8%	+13.2%	+13.9%	+10.2%	+34.8%

Sources: Gasoline index computed from average retail prices (excluding taxes), as reported by the Texas Company through June 1956 and by Platt's Oilgram Price Service for the subsequent period; other consumer price indexes from U.S. Department of Labor, Bureau of Labor Statistics.

87

TABLE VII

GASOLINE PRICES AND TAXES IN THE UNITED STATES, REGULAR GRADE GASOLINE, 1919-1964

(*Cents Per Gallon*)

Year	Tank Wagon Price (*Excluding*) Taxes	Service Station Price (*Excluding*) Taxes	State and Federal Taxes	Service Station Price (*Including*) Taxes
1964	14.82¢	19.98¢	10.37¢	30.35¢
1963	15.22	20.11	10.31	30.42
1962	15.45	20.36	10.28	30.64
1961	15.80	20.53	10.23	30.76
1960	16.08	20.99	10.14	31.13
1959	16.09	21.18	9.31	30.49
1958	16.22	21.47	8.91	30.38
1957	16.69	22.11	8.85	30.96
1956	16.32	21.57	8.36	29.93
1955	16.18	21.42	7.65	29.07
1954	16.19	21.56	7.48	29.04
1953	15.95	21.28	7.41	28.69
1952	15.27	20.24	7.32	27.56
1951	15.33	20.31	6.84	27.15
1950	15.10	20.08	6.68	26.76
1949	15.05	20.27	6.52	26.79
1948	14.55	19.54	6.34	25.88
1947	12.33	16.93	6.18	23.11
1946	10.40	14.69	6.08	20.77
1945	10.33	14.48	6.02	20.50
1944	10.49	14.62	5.97	20.59
1943	10.45	14.56	5.97	20.53
1942	10.44	14.46	5.97	20.43
1941	9.49	13.30	5.93	19.23

TABLE VII (Continued)

Year	Tank Wagon Price (Excluding) Taxes	Service Station Price (Excluding) Taxes	State and Federal Taxes	Service Station Price (Including) Taxes
1940	9.08¢	12.75¢	5.66¢	18.41¢
1939	9.58	13.31	5.44	18.75
1938	10.04	14.07	5.44	19.51
1937	10.53	14.59	5.40	19.99
1936	10.21	14.10	5.35	19.45
1935	9.73	13.55	5.29	18.84
1934	9.81	13.64	5.21	18.85
1933	9.42	12.41	5.41	17.82
1932	10.08	13.30	4.63	17.93
1931	9.65	12.98	4.00	16.98
1930	12.48	16.16	3.79	19.95
1929	14.58	17.92	3.50	21.42
1928	14.83	17.90	3.04	20.94
1927	15.00	18.28	2.81	21.09
1926	17.44	20.97	2.41	23.38
1925	17.46	20.09	2.11	22.20
1924	16.90	19.47	1.48	20.95
1923	18.66	21.06	0.91	21.97
1922	22.63	24.82	.0.38	25.20
1921	24.09	26.11	0.02	26.31
1920	28.05	29.74	0.09	29.83
1919	24.11	25.41	0.06	25.47

Source: Data for 1919-June 1956 compiled by the Texas Company; data commencing with July 1956 compiled by Platt's Oilgram Price Service.

TABLE VIII

GASOLINE PRICES AND TAXES IN MAJOR U. S. CITIES, REGULAR GRADE GASOLINE, 1964

(*Cents Per Gallon*)

City	Dealer Tank Wagon Price (*Ex. Tax*)	Service Station Price (*Ex. Tax*)	State and Federal Taxes	Service Station Price (*Incl. Tax*)
Albuquerque, N. M.	17.16	22.40	10.50	32.90
Atlanta, Ga.	16.20	21.70	10.50	32.20
Baltimore, Md.	14.53	19.24	10.58	29.82
Birmingham, Ala.	15.53	20.78	12.00	32.78
Boise, Idaho	18.75	24.82	10.00	34.82
Boston, Mass.	13.83	18.07	9.50	27.57
Buffalo, N. Y.	11.66	15.77	10.00	25.77
Burlington, Vt.	15.90	20.57	10.50	31.07
Charleston, S. C.	15.70	21.32	11.00	32.32
Charleston, W. Va.	15.03	19.48	11.00	30.48
Charlotte, N. C.	14.76	19.65	11.00	30.65
Cheyenne, Wyo.	17.72	24.65	10.00	34.65
Chicago, Ill.	14.35	20.40	9.00	29.40
Cincinnati, Ohio	14.90	19.90	11.00	30.90
Cleveland, Ohio	15.90	20.90	11.00	31.90
Dallas, Tex.	14.52	19.48	9.00	28.48
Denver, Colo.	13.50	18.90	10.00	28.90
Des Moines, Ia.	13.29	17.98	10.00	27.98
Detroit, Mich.	12.37	17.73	10.00	27.73
El Paso, Tex.	16.50	21.90	9.00	30.90

TABLE VIII (Continued)

City	Dealer Tank Wagon Price (Ex. Tax)	Service Station Price (Ex. Tax)	State and Federal Taxes	Service Station Price (Incl. Tax)
Fargo, N. D.	16.04	21.98	10.00	31.98
Great Falls, Mont.	17.68	24.13	10.00	34.13
Hartford, Conn.	12.72	16.90	10.00	26.90
Houston, Tex.	13.51	18.38	9.00	27.38
Huron, S. D.	15.85	20.40	10.00	30.40
Indianapolis, Ind.	15.08	20.73	10.00	30.73
Jackson, Miss.	16.28	22.37	12.00	34.37
Jacksonville, Fla.	16.40	21.90	11.00	32.90
Little Rock, Ark.	15.20	20.40	10.50	30.90
Los Angeles, Calif.	14.25	19.73	11.00	30.73
Louisville, Ky.	14.90	20.15	11.00	31.15
Manchester, N. H.	13.78	18.07	11.00	29.07
Memphis, Tenn.	14.13	18.98	11.00	29.98
Milwaukee, Wis.	14.00	18.98	10.00	28.98
Newark, N. J.	14.90	19.90	10.00	29.90
New Orleans, La.	13.90	18.90	11.00	29.90
New York, N. Y.	16.20	20.90	10.00	30.90
Norfolk, Va.	14.90	19.90	11.00	30.90
Omaha, Nebr.	13.93	18.82	11.00	29.82
Philadelphia, Pa.	13.49	17.65	11.00	28.65
Phoenix, Ariz.	13.80	19.32	10.00	29.32
Portland, Me.	14.25	18.65	11.00	29.65
Portland, Ore.	14.28	19.48	10.00	29.48
Providence, R. I.	12.60	16.90	11.00	27.90
Reno, Nev.	17.24	23.07	10.00	33.07

TABLE VIII (Continued)

City	Dealer Tank Wagon Price (Ex. Tax)	Service Station Price (Ex. Tax)	State and Federal Taxes	Service Station Price (Incl. Tax)
St. Louis, Mo.	13.20	18.15	9.00	27.15
Salt Lake City, Utah	15.63	21.57	10.00	31.57
San Francisco, Calif.	15.90	21.90	11.00	32.90
Seattle, Wash.	12.28	17.82	11.50	29.32
Spokane, Wash.	14.84	20.32	11.50	31.82
Tulsa, Okla.	15.03	20.57	10.50	31.07
Twin Cities, Minn.	13.36	17.98	10.00	27.98
Washington, D. C.	15.26	20.23	10.00	30.23
Wichita, Kans.	13.33	18.32	9.00	27.32
Wilmington, Del.	14.58	19.32	10.00	29.32
Average U. S.	14.82	19.98	10.37	30.35

Source: Platt's Oilgram Price Service, 1964.

TABLE IX

NUMBER AND SALES OF GASOLINE SERVICE STATIONS IN THE UNITED STATES, 1963

	Number of Service Stations	*Total Sales at Service Stations*
Alabama	4,071	$ 264,664,000
Alaska	104	15,310,000
Arizona	2,122	200,643,000
Arkansas	2,500	154,106,000
California	17,545	2,023,945,000
Colorado	2,680	219,749,000
Connecticut	2,500	247,940,000
Delaware	556	51,016,000
District of Columbia	401	68,920,000
Florida	7,782	605,480,000
Georgia	5,662	399,004,000
Hawaii	442	56,407,000
Idaho	1,083	77,291,000
Illinois	9,909	963,421,000
Indiana	6,127	529,101,000
Iowa	4,438	324,364,000
Kansas	3,468	257,234,000
Kentucky	3,674	264,123,000
Louisiana	3,207	248,557,000
Maine	1,096	85,695,000
Maryland	2,677	284,212,000
Massachusetts	4,461	419,315,000
Michigan	9,509	850,621,000
Minnesota	4,349	359,674,000
Mississippi	2,525	165,982,000

93

TABLE IX (Continued)

	Number of *Service Stations*	*Total Sales at* *Service Stations*
Missouri	5,972	$ 465,747,000
Montana	1,075	83,955,000
Nebraska	2,160	179,980,000
Nevada	555	74,504,000
New Hampshire	746	57,174,000
New Jersey	6,035	575,266,000
New Mexico	1,683	115,073,000
New York	12,010	1,135,182,000
North Carolina	6,662	421,058,000
North Dakota	799	67,375,000
Ohio	10,630	1,018,037,000
Oklahoma	3,645	257,596,000
Oregon	2,586	196,708,000
Pennsylvania	11,088	886,842,000
Rhode Island	926	66,206,000
South Carolina	3,119	198,487,000
South Dakota	1,050	79,252,000
Tennessee	4,448	335,789,000
Texas	15,069	1,023,328,000
Utah	1,340	108,630,000
Vermont	548	36,367,000
Virginia	4,624	375,523,000
Washington	3,910	297,266,000
West Virginia	2,289	146,369,000
Wisconsin	4,920	363,673,000
Wyoming	696	57,662,000
Total U. S.	211,473	$17,759,917,000

Source: U. S. Bureau of the Census.

TABLE X

MOTOR GASOLINE CONSUMPTION IN THE UNITED STATES, 1964

State	Total Gallonage
Alabama	1,173,601,000
Alaska	56,075,000
Arizona	617,131,000
Arkansas	729,755,000
California	6,915,200,000
Colorado	764,221,000
Connecticut	922,774,000
Delaware	206,598,000
District of Columbia	213,579,000
Florida	2,126,210,000
Georgia	1,563,737,000
Hawaii	160,108,000
Idaho	308,333,000
Illinois	3,506,222,000
Indiana	1,956,911,000
Iowa	1,264,294,000
Kansas	1,052,216,000
Kentucky	1,041,346,000
Louisiana	1,083,154,000
Maine	368,636,000
Maryland	1,098,212,000
Massachusetts	1,592,022,000
Michigan	3,018,362,000
Minnesota	1,451,934,000
Mississippi	768,156,000

TABLE X (Continued)

State	Total Gallonage
Missouri	1,838,699,000
Montana	313,450,000
Nebraska	676,866,000
Nevada	218,989,000
New Hampshire	233,389,000
New Jersey	2,222,915,000
New Mexico	441,606,000
New York	4,405,589,000
North Carolina	1,741,844,000
North Dakota	342,523,000
Ohio	3,523,939,000
Oklahoma	1,048,857,000
Oregon	793,407,000
Pennsylvania	3,492,876,000
Rhode Island	266,246,000
South Carolina	839,056,000
South Dakota	372,471,000
Tennessee	1,324,458,000
Texas	4,378,121,000
Utah	369,378,000
Vermont	149,728,000
Virginia	1,417,240,000
Washington	1,090,828,000
West Virginia	520,633,000
Wisconsin	1,486,269,000
Wyoming	194,451,000
Total U. S.	67,662,615,000

Source: American Petroleum Institute. Consumption excludes sales to U. S. government and sales of aviation gasoline.